Hidden Essence

Love in Deeds, Is Love indeed.

AYSHA BILQUEES

Made with ❤ on the Notion Press Platform

www.notionpress.com

Shayad is kitaab mein aapko kahin uska naam mil jaaye

Ya phir uski tareeq-e-paidaish ka koi nishaan mil jaaye

Uske adaab-o-aadat pe koi kalaam mil jaaye

Duaon se jo likha ho waisa koi anjaam mil jaaye

- Aysha Bilquees

Contents

CONTENTS

Preface

It's very hard to get me to work - unless I have a khurafat in my mind.
This book is the result of one such khurafati idea that struck me during a particularly boring lecture. While most books are named after the ideas they carry, this one's different. Here, the idea itself was built around the name: *Hidden Essence.*

This phrase has intrigued me for years. The first time I heard those two words, I paused. *Essence?* That's the soul of something. How can that be hidden? How can someone hide essence - of all things? That thought clung to me, tugged at the corners of my mind. Until one random day, sitting between Shruti and Aparna, without even having Mentos, *"mere dimagh ki batti jal gayi."*

And I realized: Hidden essence is never really hidden.
It's just quietly present, always waiting to be felt.

And love - real love - is the truest essence of all. It's not always loud, filtered, or perfectly timed. It's in the unnoticed, the unsaid. It's in the silence between shared glances. It's in the comfort of simply being there. And honestly? It's rarely sane.

It's in your dad stacking crates of mangoes just because you said you liked them once.
It's in your mom making aalu ki bhujia for those bemurawwat aulaads who don't eat meat.
It's in someone remembering you've changed your specs even after being years apart.
It's when your friends don't eat in front of you while you're

fasting.

It's in waiting for the song to finish before saying goodbye, just to steal a few more moments together.

It's sitting in silence - not because you have nothing to say, but because the silence itself feels full.

It's in the hand that quietly fixes your scarf.

It's in someone silently keeping a seat for you every single time.

It's in those little, almost invisible acts - each one quietly saying: *You matter.*

You just have to look.

And more than anything, love hides in the eyes.
Always, in the eyes.

No, it's not always butterflies.
It's not always smooth.
But it's peace.
It's calm in the storm.
It's chaos wrapped in quiet care.
It's love in its rawest, most honest form.
It's *Hidden Essence*.

This book is a collection of those silences, those stares, those in-between spaces where love lives without a name; where we embrace the thoughts that never become words.

To the mangoes,
to the saved seats,
to the soft "I'm here" without saying it.

To the Hidden Essence - of people, of emotions, of moments.

Welcome to its world.

I hope you find yourself in these pages.

Acknowledgments

To those who shared their stories, their intimate moments with me...

To Riddhi, for helping me bring the cover to life.

And above all -
To the One who gifted me this strange ability to feel deeply, to find beauty in the quiet, to notice too much, and somehow put it into words.
For every word that found its way here - it was never really mine. Every word belongs to You, Almighty.

You have held me through,

I hope you always do

AAHAT

1. Alam-e-Arwah

Alam-e-Arwah (Realm of Souls) is the place where all souls were created by Allah - a divine sanctuary where they resided before being sent into this physical world. It's said that souls connected there carry an unexplainable bond into this life - a bond so profound and surreal that it defies logic, words, and even the limits of your understanding.

How do you explain something so strange?
That they were never strangers, not even when you met them for the first time.
That you somehow knew the exact color of the kurta they'd wear on a festival without any reason.
Or that a sudden thought crossed your mind - they'll be in this room - only to find them standing there the next moment, as if the universe whispered it into your soul.

At first, it feels like an illusion, a trick of your mind - but it's not. Or at least, you think it's not.

And then there are those prayers - when their name escapes your lips without warning.
"Ya Allah, protect them," you whisper, wondering why you suddenly prayed for them...
Only to later discover they needed that protection, that prayer, at that very moment.
The connection feels too precise, too overwhelming - like your soul knows something your mind doesn't.

But what if?
What if it is just your mind playing games?
What if they have no idea about any of this - no idea that you

sense them, think of them, or feel this unspoken connection?
What if all this is one-sided, nothing more than a fabrication of
your own imagination?
It terrifies you to even consider it.

And no, it isn't love.
It's not the butterflies-in-your-stomach kind of feeling.
It's not romance, infatuation, or longing.
It's something far stranger, deeper, and harder to define.
It's like your soul recognizes them at a level that words cannot
describe -
Yet your heart is too scared to admit it out loud.

It scares you so much that your hands are trembling as you
write this,
Gripping the bedsheets tightly because the weight of this
connection is too much to bear.
You want to block them from every platform,
Erase them from your thoughts,
Never hear their name again - just to escape this storm inside
you.

And yet, at the same time,
You're thankful it's them.
Because you know, deep down,
They would never hurt you,
Never wish anything bad for you.

You're torn -
Terrified they might think it's insane if they ever knew.
Afraid they'd laugh, or dismiss it as childish,
When for you, it's so real it consumes you.

You wonder if it's better to stay silent forever,
Because the risk of being misunderstood is too great.

And yet...
You cannot shake it.
Maybe this connection truly began in Alam-e-Arwah -
A spiritual thread tying your souls together in a way that
transcends time and space.
Or maybe, just maybe, it's all in your head.
Either way, the fear, the confusion, and the intensity are real.
And you don't know whether to run from it, embrace it, or
simply let it be.

What do you do?
You don't know...
It's so heavy on your heart.
At first, you thought it was just friendship.
But the truth is - you have better friends than them.
You've had deeper, more meaningful friendships with others.

But somehow...
It doesn't feel the same.
The connection with them feels different.
It's so much more complex, so much more overwhelming -
And you don't know how to handle it.
You don't know how to let go,
Or even if you should.

But no...
You don't want it to be two-sided.
You don't want them to feel the same,
Because the fear of them thinking you're insane is too much to
bear.
You just want them to remain unaware,

To think of you as just another person in their life -
Not someone consumed by a connection they can't even
fathom.

But then again...
What if it is two-sided?
What if they feel the same way,
But they're just too scared to admit it too?
What if all this time,
We've been walking around with the same thoughts, the same
feelings -
Never daring to speak them?

2. Were We Ever Strangers?

Were we ever strangers?

Haven't I known you forever?

Don't tell me we were strangers before our eyes met and our hearts synchronized.

Can strangers fit together flawlessly, like long-lost puzzle pieces?

Can strangers feel as if they are eight years old together?

Do they run around like toddlers, tease like siblings, argue like partners,

and lose themselves in each other's eyes?

Can they finish sentences and understand silence?

Do they understand thoughts at a glance?

Do they share vulnerable moments without fear of scrutiny?

Have a subconscious connection that is beyond words and logic and feels like destiny?

Do strangers dream the same dream at midnight.

Do they reach for the same star, or write parallel lines in different diaries.

Do strangers breathe in sync while miles apart,

or find poetry in each other's pauses.

Do they remember things they never lived together,

or feel nostalgia for a life they're still building.

Do strangers have a passion that ignites their souls

when they see a reflection of themselves in the eyes of another?

Do they feel at home with each other

and believe they were destined to meet in this huge world?

Do they realize, that they, were never truly STRANGERS?

3. Where I'm meant to be

Lemme hold you by your arms and lean on your shoulder.
You take a few seconds to realize what just happened, look at
me with a side eye, and then, gently, you lean your head on
mine.
And as we both close our eyes, our lips curve into soft smiles,
and our hearts overflow with contentment.

Can I?
May I?
Would you reciprocate the way you do in my dreams?

Ohh... it's been ages since I last held you, but this time, it would
be different.
Everything has changed - we have changed, the feelings have
changed - yet somehow, everything still feels the same.
The soft corner we've always had for each other remains
untouched.
The passion between us, the understanding, the unsaid promise
we have kept for years, and the way we can share anything and
everything -
Without fear of judgment, without thinking twice.

The way I speak to you is the way I talk to myself -
Or maybe even better.
I love talking, but the passion I have when I talk to you is
different.
I want to tell you everything -
From how pigeons always build nests on my balcony
To the way I talk to God.

And you listen to me so patiently -
Not that I leave you with any other option -
But you don't just listen to what I say,
You retain it.

And even though I never show it,
I remember everything you've ever said and done.
I notice the way you've looked at me and at others.
I took note of how you like your food less spicy
And which fresh juice you prefer.
I know the way you frown
And how you get vertical lines on your lips when you're upset.

I miss listening to everything you've got to say -
From how you got to know about that new brand
To what's the most annoying habit of your roommate.
I want to listen to everything you have to say.

You've always felt like home.
And maybe that's why - no matter how much time passes -
The warmth of you still feels so familiar.

I want you to hold my hands.
Would you?
What would it feel like to intertwine our fingers?
To feel the gentle press of your palm against mine -
As if every space between my fingers was always meant to fit
yours?
I imagine it would feel like grounding myself in something safe,
something real.
Like holding the universe in my hands and knowing it's all mine.

Can I lean my back on your chest,
Hearing the rhythm of your heartbeat?

I'd wonder how thinking about something so simple could give
me shivers.
Your arms around me,
Your breath steady against my skin,
And that unshakable feeling that this - this - is where I'm meant
to be.

But... would this always remain just a dream?
Would these moments, these feelings, ever find their way into
reality?
Or am I destined to only live them in the quiet corners of my
mind,
Where everything is perfect, but nothing is real?

Tell me -
Will I ever be able to hold you like this,
To live this dream,
Or will it forever remain a whispered wish,
Lost in the echoes of my heart?

Because if this is just a dream...
I don't think I ever want to wake up.

4. Intezaar!

Intezaar! Aur kitna intezaar karu uska?
One line answer?
Jab tak woh khaas se aam na ho jaaye...

The reason you wait for someone isn't them - it's you.
Because no one else makes you feel the way they do.
Your heart doesn't race when someone else looks at you.
Your world doesn't pause when someone else laughs like them,
speaks like them.
They are out of the equation now -
It's just you and your love.

So, the simple answer?
Love them with everything you have. But let it be yours alone.
Don't chase them. Don't.
Don't let them know they still have a place inside you.
Don't let them control your emotions, your day, your peace.
Don't be the person who answers their call at odd hours,
Who becomes available just because they have no one else
around.

But love them in ways they've never been loved before.
In ways that bring them peace - even from a distance.
Hug them with your prayers.
Pray for their dreams like they're your own.
Pray that they never lie awake at 2 AM, staring at the ceiling,
wondering what went wrong.

Pray that when they find love, it is kind to them.
And pray that love is yours.
Pray that if, by some miracle, you both find your way back to each other -
You cherish, love, and respect one another the way you both deserve.
And this time, you make it last.

Write down the things you wish you could tell them.
Write it all.
How you know the exact expression they'll make before you even crack a joke?
How you look at the moon and hope they're looking at it too.
How you hug your pillow tighter when you miss them.
How your hand pauses mid-meal when you taste masala kulcha from that one restaurant.
How just seeing a backpack can take you back in time.
Tuck those words away in a diary - hidden, where they'll never find them.
Maybe one day, when you both share the same bookshelf,
They'll be searching for a book...
And end up picking it up.
And maybe - just maybe - they'll know.

Till then...
Do it all.
But do it in silence.
Until one day...
That diary becomes just another notebook.
You don't remember the sound of their laugh anymore.
That song plays, and it doesn't remind you of them.
They just become another person.

Kyuki intezaar sirf tab tak hota hai, jab tak woh khaas se aam na ho jae

15

Kyuki intezaar sirf tab tak hota hai, jab tak woh khaas se aam na ho jae

5. Grown Apart

One day, you'll wake up and realize that the person who once felt like your whole world now feels... distant.
Not because of a fight, not because you wanted them to be, but because life happened.
Time stretched between you like an ocean, pulling you into separate currents, until one day you looked up and they weren't right beside you anymore.

Before you knew it, the little details - their favorite song, the way they laughed at your worst jokes - started slipping away.
You'll try to remember, you'll wonder when the daily conversations turned into occasional check-ins, when their voice became something you had to remember rather than something you heard every day.
You'll try to pinpoint the exact moment when they stopped being the first person you told everything to.

And it'll hurt - not in a sharp, unbearable way, but in the kind that lingers.
The kind that sits quietly in the background of your mind, making you miss them in moments you don't expect.
Like when you hear a joke and instinctively think of them, only to realize they're not there to share it with.
Or when you visit a place you both loved, and suddenly, the air feels too heavy with memories.

You'll think about how they were once your person for everything - the good news, the bad news, the meaningless updates - and now, you hesitate before dialing, wondering if they'll still pick up the same way.

Wondering if you still have the right to reach out, or if time has silently revoked that privilege.

On the surface, everything has changed.
You both have new routines, new people, new lives that no longer intertwine the way they once did.
You no longer know the little things - how their taste in music has evolved, what keeps them up at night, what they think about before they fall asleep.
There are gaps now, spaces that used to be filled with endless words and effortless understanding.

You have learned to live without them, and they have learned to live without you.
And yet, somehow, when you do talk, it doesn't feel unfamiliar.
There's no awkwardness, no need for explanations.
The silences between you aren't empty; they're full - of memories, of understanding, of a bond that time couldn't erase.
It's in the way their voice still carries the comfort of old times, in the way their presence still feels like a safe harbor, even after all the years apart.
It's in the way neither of you ever have to ask, *Where did we go wrong?* because deep down, you both know you never did.

Superficially, everything is different - you have changed, they have changed, the world around you has changed - but at the core of it all, the essence of what you were to each other remains untouched.
They still bring you the same kind of peace.
They still feel like home.
And even though you don't know each other in the same way anymore, you're not strangers.

You're just two people who grew up, took different roads, but never really let go.

Because the peace you both have spent years searching for - in people, in places, in fleeting moments that never quite felt enough - was always right here, in each other.
In the way their presence still feels like a place you know by heart,
In the way, even after everything, they are still the person you think of when the world feels too loud.
You may have outgrown the version of yourselves that once knew every little thing about each other,
But somehow, in ways neither of you can explain, you never stopped belonging.

LAMS

6. Name

They say you love the sound of your name when it rolls off the lips of someone you love. That it becomes the sweetest melody, a lullaby you never tire of hearing.
But mine??? Doesn't take my name.
He just doesn't.
I can count on my fingers the number of times he's actually said it - once, maybe twice. That too he would say my full name. And I remember things when they're about him. Every detail, every moment, every glance is etched into my mind like poetry on an old, treasured parchment.

So, what does he call me?
Honestly, nothing!!!
Neither my name nor a pet name, a nickname, just... nothing.
People give names to the ones they love. It's an act of belonging, of carving a special space in their world for someone.
Then why doesn't he call me something?
Is it all in my head? A cruel trick of my own making?
Is this love truly one-sided?
No. It isn't.
Because he addresses me in ways so unique, so intimate, that words seem unnecessary.

He screams my name with his eyes.
When I'm looking away, he keeps his gaze on me, steady, burning, until I feel its heat crawling up my skin. Until my breath catches, and I have no choice but to turn, to meet those dark, knowing eyes that hold a thousand unspoken things.
When he needs my attention, he doesn't call out. He simply extends his hand, palm open, forefinger slightly distant from the

other three fingers - silent, certain. And when my fingers touch his, he pulls me closer, makes me sit beside him, as if that was where I was always meant to be. Only then does he begin to talk, as if my presence is the missing puzzle piece his words needed before they could exist.

And when he speaks about me in a room full of people? He doesn't say my name. He doesn't have to.
Instead, he says
"ye"
"Ye ladki"
"Vo"
"Vaha jo khadi hai"
His eyes flicker toward me, his gaze lingers, and it's only when someone else - some clueless bystander - finally utters my name that he acknowledges it. As if the world itself needed to confirm my existence before he would.

But people name what's theirs. And if I have no name in his world, what does that make me?
And do you think that bothers me? Do you think I lie awake at night, aching for him to say my name?
Nahh!! Not even a bit.
Because my name is for everyone else to say. But the way he addresses me? That's just for him and me.
When he pulls my hand instead of calling me, it feels like a secret language only we understand. When he locks his gaze with mine, I hear my name louder than any word could ever convey. When he refuses to say it aloud, it's not neglect - it's a possession too deep, too intimate, too his to be reduced to mere syllables.

And once in a blue moon, when he says my name. He says it in the weirdest accent possible. The way he says la"saag"na - like it's some foreign word he can't quite get right. He stretches it out, exaggerates it, and makes it sound so utterly ridiculous. ufff.. And now? Now, I can never pronounce *lasagna* properly again.

And yet - when I'm not around...
When in the quiet of the night he's talking about me to someone who doesn't know me - what then?
Ohhh... What does he say about me?
Does he say my name? Does it taste different in his mouth when I'm not there to hear it?
Do his eyes light up the way they do when he looks at me?
Do his cheeks turn red like ripe tamatar the way they do when he blushes in front of me?
Does he start looking here and there, flustered, unable to meet their gaze, just so they don't catch him blushing?
I wish I knew. I wish I could see him in those moments.
But even if he never says my name, I know - I just know - that when he speaks of me, I am there in his voice, in the way his lips curve ever so slightly, in the warmth that sneaks into his words and cheeks like an unspoken confession.
And maybe, just maybe, that's more than enough.

7. Held By His Love

How much must a man have loved a woman that every time he looked at her, his eyes welled up - not once, not twice, but again and again? It wasn't just admiration, nor was it mere attachment. It was something deeper, something that made silence heavy and glances sacred. The glistening tear in his deep black eyes wasn't an accident - it was a prayer that had found its answer, a longing that had finally been granted form.

She had always dismissed it, thinking it was just her imagination. Perhaps the light reflected strangely, making his eyes appear damp. Perhaps she was overanalyzing fleeting moments. But the day her own eyes welled up while meeting his gaze, she realized - this wasn't a trick of the mind. This wasn't a coincidence.

She felt it.

She felt the weight of every unsaid word, every moment he had spent loving her in silence. It was as if his heart had been carrying a love so vast, so patient, that even the universe had taken notice. And when she looked back at him, something inside her stirred - an ache, a knowing, an overwhelming realization.

Agar ye naimat hai to sirf usse hi kyun?
Agar ajar hai to bepanaah hai.

How could she rise from a prostration of gratitude when she had been given everything - more than she had ever asked for, more than she had even dared to desire? It terrified her. Not the love itself, but its depth. Its purity. Its undeniability.

She had heard of love that demands, love that consumes, love that suffocates. But this... this was love that only knew how to give. A love that expected nothing in return, yet existed so fiercely that even the air around them carried its presence.

She wondered how long he had waited, how many nights he had spent whispering her name into the void, how many times he had let his heart break just so he could love her without asking for anything back. How many prayers had risen to the heavens with her name woven between them?

Vo shukar ke sajde se uthe kaise,
Usse sab kuch dedia gaya tha,
Jitna usne manga tha usse kahin zyada,
Jitne ki khawahish kya vo andaaza v nahi laga sakti thi.

And yet, even after realizing this, she never told him. She never let him know that his love had reached her heart. But wasn't that how some prayers worked? The one who asked never truly knew how far they traveled, how deeply they were answered.

She found herself thinking of him at odd moments, in spaces he had never even entered. She would catch a glimpse of something - a song playing in the background, a phrase someone said, the way the evening sun fell on the pavement - and suddenly, there he was. Not in presence, but in essence.

She began to notice things she had never paid attention to before. The way his voice would soften when he spoke her name. The way his hands curled into fists, as if holding himself back from reaching out. The way he never let his emotions burden her, even when they filled the room like unshed rain.

And then, there were the moments that truly shook her.

The time he stayed back in the cold, making sure she got home safely, without her even asking. The time he prayed for her before praying for himself. The time she caught him staring at her - not with expectation, not with hope, but with something deeper. Something quieter. As if loving her was the most natural thing he had ever done, as if he had accepted, long ago, that even if she never loved him back, he would never know how to stop.

She had never known a love like this.

A love that expected no grand reciprocation.
A love that stayed, even in the shadows.
A love that never asked for her attention, yet never wavered when it had it.

So, when she loses sleep at night, when she finds herself murmuring a prayer for him in the quiet hours, it is not just because she loves him.

It's because his love created a place in her heart without them even knowing.
It's because his pure intentions seeped into her soul like whispered prayers carried by the wind.
It's because love like his does not pass through life unnoticed.

And oh, she is thankful - with every ounce of her existence.

Thankful for the door she never thought was hers to open.
Thankful for the feelings she never knew she was capable of holding.
Thankful, because somewhere between his silent prayers and her unconscious gratitude, they had both become proof that love - true, unwavering, selfless love - exists.

He did nothing, yet he did everything.

And now, she carries the weight of it - the quiet, unshaken love that asked for nothing but gave everything.

She feels it in the silence between heartbeats.
In the prayers that rise from her lips before she even realizes she is saying his name.
In the way her soul recognizes something it never sought, yet now cannot imagine life without.

Because love like his does not just touch a heart - it awakens it.
It moves the heavens.
It bends the universe.
It turns an ordinary life into a story whispered in the language of fate.

And she understands now.

She understands what it means to be the answer to someone's deepest, most sacred plea.
She understands that love like this is not given - it is bestowed.
That to be loved like this is not just a blessing - it is proof that some prayers are heard long before they are spoken.

And with that understanding, she bows her head in gratitude.

Because she was not just loved.
She was chosen over and over again.

8. Essence of YOU

I wanna stay,

Just be there,

Sit quietly beside you,

Not because I have nothing to say,

But because with you, silence feels enough.

I wanna hold your hand,

Not just to feel your warmth,

But to remind you-on days when your strength falters,

That you don't have to face anything alone.

I wanna talk gibberish,

Say things that make no sense,

Make up words only we understand,

And laugh until our stomach hurts-

Because nothing feels as light as being lost in you.

I wanna put my head on your shoulder,

Close my eyes and just breathe you in,

Feel your heartbeat beneath my cheek,

And fall asleep in the Essence of you.

I wanna fall asleep to the sound of your breath,

Wake up in the middle of the night,

Turn towards you in the dim light,

And find you already looking at me-

Like I am something precious,

Something you don't ever want to look away from.

I don't want the moon or the stars,

I don't need riches or kingdoms.

I want something far more precious and rarer

I want YOU

I wanna just BE with you-

Not just in the grand, magical moments,

But in the everyday ones.

In the lazy Sunday mornings,

The hurried Monday chaos,

The tired midweek evenings when all we do is exist in the same space.

I wanna hold your hand on the days that break you,

Squeeze it tighter when words fail,

Be your calm in the storm,

Be your home when everything else feels foreign.

I wanna stand beside you when you need a partner,

Behind you when you need support,

Ahead of you if anything dares to harm you.

I wanna brush my nose against yours,

Be so close that my eyelashes touch yours,

Feel your breath mix with mine,

Erase every space, every line.

I wanna watch you laugh,

Memorize the way your eyes shine,

The way your lips twitch before a smile,

The way your voice softens when you look at me say "ae"

I wanna fight with you,

Not because I want to,

But because love isn't about never arguing-

It's about knowing that no matter what,

No matter how hard the conversation,

No matter how stubborn we both are,

We will always choose each other in the end.

I wanna dream with you,

Talk about the future like we already own it,

Like time bends to our love,

Like the universe is merely waiting for us to step into it together.

I wanna wake up to you,

Not just tomorrow,

Not just for now,

But for as long as time will allow.

I wanna grow old with you,

Watch your beautiful hands wrinkle, (They would still be beautiful to me)

Watch our hair turn silver, (if there's any left on our heads)

Watch our love remain untouched by time.

I wanna sit with you on a cold winter morning,

Drink Kanji with you as the sun spills golden light over your face,

And think to myself-

'There's nowhere else I'd rather be.'

I wanna dance with you in the kitchen,

Barefoot, no music,

Just my laughter, just your heartbeat,

Just us.

I wanna spend rainy days curled up with you,

Tracing my fingers over your face,

Memorizing the shape of your smile,

Like it's the only thing that matters.

I wanna read books with you,

Sit beside you with my legs over yours,

Look up every once in a while,

Just to catch you looking at me.

I wanna whisper my dreams to you at midnight,

Lay my head against your chest,

And listen to the steady sound of your breath.

I wanna love you in all the ways love was meant to be felt.

In the loud moments, in the quiet ones,

In the easy days, in the difficult ones.

Not just when it's convenient,

Not just when it's simple,

But always.

I don't need the whole world.

I don't need forever if it isn't with you.

I just want YOU.

9. Just "By the way" Friends

I don't usually remember details,

not what I was wearing,

not even what day it was.

But that day?

It stayed.

I've written five poems on that day,

and still, it doesn't feel enough.

You'd just finished your performance,

standing there with a girl

who probably had zero interest in you,

and you,

you were just being polite,

conversing,

smiling,

nothing more.

And yet,

I don't know what snapped in me,

what surged,

what sparked,

what made me do it.

I walked up,

held your hand,

just held it,

no warning,

no context,

no reason.

Started speaking nonsense,

because my heart

was louder than my tongue could translate.

It wasn't even jealousy,

it was an urge

to be near you.

And you,

you looked at me,

stunned.

You weren't listening at first,

But your eyes,

they softened.

I don't remember when the girl walked away,

no goodbye,

no question,

just gone.

And I swear,

I felt bad for her,

still do,

for how I interrupted,

for how you didn't even look back.

But maybe we both knew,

neither of us were in control of what happened.

We don't act like this,

you and I,

we never did.

You had changed by then,

the kurta gone,

replaced with a t-shirt that looked good.

And I,

without thinking,

asked,

why did you change,

as if you needed my permission.

And then we walked,

down that corridor,

still holding both hands,

mine in yours,

yours in mine,

like we'd done it forever,

like the world wasn't watching.

People passed us,

some stared,

some raised their brows.

And why wouldn't they,

But we didn't care,

our steps were slow,

voices low,

fingers folded like a secret.

We walked

until we reached the end of the corridor.

And then,

my friends,

started calling me back,

waking me from a dream

I hadn't realized I'd slipped into.

So, I turned to you and said,

go home, change into that kurta again, then come back,

as a joke,

but more, as a wish.

And I walked away.

Little did I know,

you would actually go and change.

And now,

when people claim they love me,

I tell them,

go change into the kurta.

No one ever does.

No one should.

Because even if they did,

I'd still be thinking of you.

10. Ladies Washroom

She entered the room a little early that day,

carrying a silence louder than anything around her.

She didn't want to talk.

Didn't want to smile.

She just... wanted to disappear.

Something inside her felt heavy-

and no, she wouldn't have been able to explain it if someone asked.

So, she slipped away to the last bench,

hoping the room would forget she even existed.

No greetings, no small talk-

just space.

Just a quiet corner to breathe.

But his eyes followed her.

And so did he.

He called her,

and when she gave that little sign

I'm okay here,

he didn't push.

He just showed up.

Sat beside her

And then this Human started ...

"Kya hua hai, bol?"

"Bol, bol..."

He threw in those dumb jokes.

The kind that aren't even funny-

but they're so him, she smiled.

Involuntarily.

She kept brushing him off.

Told him she needed space.

Tried to sound firm.

He nodded like he understood-

but didn't move.

Just stayed.

Like some people do-

not because they didn't hear you,

but because they did.

A few minutes passed like that.

Then came:

"Kuch nahi hua hai toh chal."

"Chal, aage."

Over and over.

She groaned internally and got up.

'Yeh nahi chodega ab.'

She walked to the front and sat down.

Some time later, she stood up to leave the class-

just to breathe a little.

And of course,

the jin got activated again 'Kidhar?' he asked.

She sighed and came up with the best excuse to get away,

'washroom'

Thinking, he'd let her be now.

Or maybe ask a girl to go with her.

Which would've been fine.

But him?

He said, "Chal… hum bhi chal rahe hain saath mein."

You know that inner urge to hit your head against a wall?

Yeah. In the moment she felt that.

She rolled her eyes behind his back and followed him.

But somewhere, quietly…

something inside her softened.

Because-

who does that?

He walked with her.

Didn't talk much.

Didn't try to make it a moment.

He just walked.

When they reached the washroom,

she handed him her phone and walked in.

Inside, she stood in front of the mirror.

Looked at herself.

Tried to understand-

was she really someone people would do so much for?

Was she really... worth waiting outside a ladies' washroom for,

without any reason?

And when she stepped out,

there he was-walking in the corridor,

not scrolling through his phone,

not looking bored,

just... being there.

"Chale?" he asked.

As if she had been the one waiting for him.

She never forgot that day.

Not because anything big happened.

But because of everything small that did.

Because even in the middle of her storm,

he never tried to drag her out.

He didn't force her to be okay.

He just stood beside her-

quiet, and steady.

And somehow,

that was enough.

Enough to remind her-

she wasn't alone.

That even when she asked for space,

there is someone who'll make sure...

she never really has to feel it.

11. Jealousy

I saw it in your urgency-
The way your hand reached out, instantly,
Snatching my phone before thoughts could even form,
As if guarding your place from an approaching storm.

Your eyes raced across the glowing screen,
Searching for a face you feared unseen.
The man on my wallpaper, still and framed-
You hunted for a story, for a threat unnamed.

And oh-
the breath you didn't know you held
was slowly, gently, quietly expelled.
A sigh of relief, your tension undone,
When you saw - he was just someone.
A stranger. A Celeb. Not my fate
Not someone you would really hate.

I saw it again in your dipped voice,
When you asked,
"Koi aur hai kya?"
As if my verses could belong to another,
As if my metaphors weren't already drenched in you, my lover.

And i said yes

It pinched you-
I saw it show.
You acted cool, but I still know.
Your eyes - oh love, they always tell,
Even when your lips wear silence well.

Hidden Essence

And I swear,

Those are your only aches that make me smile,
When you stumble in jealousy for a while.
Because in that ache, your love shines through-
More honest than any whispered I love you.

Don't ask me how I held back tight,
From pulling you close in that day light.
To plant reassurances on your worried face,
And hold you till your doubts leave without a trace.

But instead, I let silence hum between,
Let comfort bloom in the space unseen.
Let my heart whisper, slow and true:
"It's always been you. Just you."

Even when I didn't yet believe,
Even when I made myself grieve,
Even when my lips refused to speak,
My soul bent toward you, soft and weak.

You'll never know the war I fought,
To calm your storms, to guard your thought.
To cup your face and softly say:
"No poem was ever meant to stray."

My words are yours, my silence too,
Every shade my heart turns to.
Every beat I try to hide,
Every prayer I send at night.

It's you.
It's always been.
In every noise, in every quiet

In all I share and all I don't,
In what I say, and what I won't.

You live in rhythm, in metaphor,
In every ache I can't ignore.
In all the spaces unexplained,
Where only you remain - unnamed.

12. The Kurta Attack

I entered the corridor, which was busier than usual-

full of people and conversations I can't even remember now.

I was talking to a friend about something forgettable.

And I did forget,

just seconds later,

when I saw YOU.

You were standing at a distance,

laughing at something someone had said,

wearing a kurta in a colour I still can't name-

somewhere between light blue and grey,

like the sky just before it begins to rain.

I've never been good with colours,

but you...

you looked like something I can never quite put into words.

And the strangest part?

We weren't even on talking terms.

There was distance-unspoken, unexplained.

A quiet cold war we never declared but both felt.

So, when I raised my hand, smiled wide,

and signed an exaggerated little arrow shooting through my heart-

it was unexpected.

Playful, yes.

Dramatic, yes.

But honest.

So painfully, stupidly honest.

You weren't expecting it.

Neither was I.

You turned toward me,

just a little caught off guard.

And then,so gently,

you reached out,

not hesitating, not uncertain

and held my hand.

Slow, but sure.

The way you always do.

Not in passing.

Not like friends do.

You HELD it.

I was still recovering from the kurta attack

when our eyes met.

And oh-those eyes.

Lined softly with surma,

as if they needed more intensity.

But they didn't just look at me-

they rested on me.

Like they had been waiting.

Like I was something they were finally allowed to see.

You looked at me like there was no one else in that corridor.

Like time had folded around us.

I kept talking-

partly trying to convince my heart that we were JUST friends,

partly hoping the moment wouldn't break.

I don't even remember what I said.

Jokes, maybe. Little nothings meant for everyone.

But you kept looking.

You said a word or two, barely.

You just stood there, still holding my hand-

like you didn't want the moment to move.

Neither did I.

It was warm.

Like homes are.

I didn't even realise we had created a bubble

until I noticed the glances-

a couple of friends watching,

smiling too knowingly.

And suddenly, I remembered where we were.

What we weren't supposed to be.

So I smiled,

the way people do when they're trying to be normal again,

gently pulled my hand away,

wished you luck,

and walked past.

But even as I walked away,

I could still feel the warmth of your hand lingering in mine,

and the quiet heat of your gaze on my back.

And I think...
some part of me never really let go.
It stayed there,

in that corridor,

in the arms of a colour, I still can't name.

WISAAL

13. You Are the Death of Me

You are the death of me.

No, quite literally.

See, I spent years being the voice of reason-

Telling people, "Love? That's just a season."

"Be practical. Logical. Make a pros-and-cons sheet.

Choose a partner like a bank loan-secure and neat."

I believed in stability over spark,

Sanity over butterflies in the dark.

In the kind of love that doesn't shake you,

That doesn't have the power to break you.

I preached calm love. Quiet love.

The one that doesn't steal your sleep.

Not the kind that robs your peace,

Or hugs your ribs too tight to breathe.

I said:

"Think with your head. Don't die for love-

Be mature! No one does that anymore.

If they're kind, if they care, if they reply fast..

Then that's enough. That's fair."

And I meant it.

Till YOU happened.

Till your love crawled beneath my skin

And rewrote every rule I believed in.

Your name began skipping inside my chest,

Like even my heart couldn't rest.

My friends-

They say I've changed.

That my eyes shine when I talk about this man.

They say they've never seen me like this-

The girl who blushes at her own diary entries,

Who giggles now like a five-year-old kid,

Who randomly smiles at walls,

Who suddenly believes in love after all.

I had a part of her in me once-

But I'd killed her, quite literally.

Yet this time, she's emerged stronger.

She's soft and fierce.

Silly.

Hopeless.

True.

Delusional.

She sits alone in her room,

Blushing like she's being teased-

Except no one's there.

Just the thought of you,

Hovering in the air.

And God.

The way she speaks to God about you-

She's turned her prayers into love confessions.

Nightly updates. Endless sessions.

She tells Him how adorable your nose is,

How you throw back your neck when you laugh

How her Humpty Dumpty always falls and breaks himself.

She could write entire scriptures

On the way you raise your eyebrows.

And every night, she ends the same-

Let me keep him. Please.

Let me keep him forever.

Because now, I don't want calculated love.

I don't want safe.

I want this.

The wild. The magical. The soul-shaking bliss.

The messy, irrational,

"I-will-die-a-little-inside-if-I-lose-this" kind.

The kind I swore I'd never believe in.

The kind that made me eat my words

But now?

Now my friends are after me-

"Practice what you preach" they laugh.

"Where's your logic? Where's your brain? Your famous checklist?"

And honestly? I'd run.

But I'm too busy writing you another poem.

You-

You are the death of who I was.

And somehow,

The beginning of every poem

I never thought I'd write.

The heartbeat I didn't know I was missing.

The prayer I never knew I'd keep repeating.

The truth that finally

Made a liar out of my logic.

You are the death of me.

But oh-

What a way to live.

14. Through All the Mess

I see how people get defensive when I do this.
 How their voice go up the moment I gently point out
something.
 How they pull away, shut down, feel like I'm attacking - even
when I'm not.
 So with most people, I've learned to stop.
 I stay quiet now.
 I let them figure things out on their own.
 I smile, I nod, I keep my observations to myself.
 Not because I don't care - but because not everyone knows
how to receive care that doesn't sound like praise.

Because the truth is: when I correct, it's never to judge.
 I don't say it to feel superior.
 I don't say it to tear anyone down.
 I say it because I care enough to notice.

But with you...
 It'll be different.
 With you, I won't stay silent.
 I won't watch you mess up and just stand by, smiling politely.
 With you, I'll speak.
 I'll gently say the things I swallow with everyone else..
 Because I'll trust you enough to believe you'll hear my heart
behind my words.
 Because I'll know that you'll know - I'm always on your team.

Through all this Mess, Always.

I won't correct you to control you.
 I won't point things out to make you feel small.

It'll never be about proving I'm right or keeping score.
It'll simply be because you'll matter to me too much to let
things sit and rot in silence.
 Because I'll want you to grow, I'll want us to grow, and I'll
believe we can handle even the uncomfortable parts - together.

And even though I know you'll probably understand my heart
anyway, I'll still say it.
 Because I'll never want you to doubt where I'm coming from.

So if one day, I stop you mid-conversation and say:
 "You know... maybe you could've handled that a little
differently."
 Or if I slip it in while stealing food off your plate.
 While you're tying your shoelaces.
 While we're sitting quietly, waiting for lasagna to arrive.
 While I'm fixing your hoodie.
 While we're walking home and the street's a little too quiet.
 Know that I won't be doing it to embarrass you.
 I won't be trying to pull you down.
 I won't be trying to make you feel any less.

It'll only be because I care enough to say the thing that's hard to
say.
 Because I'll trust you to hold my honesty softly - the way I'll
hold you.

I've seen how people love sometimes.
 How they shout.
 How they belittle.
 How they punish with silence.
 How they talk behind backs.
 How they vent to everyone except the person who matters.
 And I've never understood that.

I don't want that.
I won't do that.

When I love, I won't destroy.
 I won't vent about you to others.
 I'll sit beside you, even when it's messy, and I'll say:
 "Hey, this thing... let's do better next time. You and me."

That'll be love for me.
 Not pretending everything's perfect.
 Not running away from the hard parts.
 But holding the hard parts gently.
 Sitting safely inside the hard conversations because I'll believe
we're strong enough for it.

So, if I ever bring up something you don't want to hear,
 If I ever say something that makes you pause -
 Know that I'm not attacking you.
 I'm loving you.
 I'm choosing us.
 I'm protecting us.

And you'll get to do the same with me too.
 You'll pull me aside and say:
 "You slipped here. But I've got you."
And even in the cracks I show,

Your love will stay, and I will know....

15. The Price Tag on Feelings

You know what breaks my heart a little?

How gifts have somehow turned into calculations.

I see people talk about the price of what they gave or got.
 At weddings, I've watched families write names and amounts in little registers -
 "So we'll know what to return when it's their turn."
 And every time, something inside me just... wilts.

Because I've never known how to do that math.

For me, gifts were never supposed to be about the money.
 They were supposed to be about the person.
 About the thought that led you to pick something and say,
 "This reminded me of you."

You could get me something outrageously expensive -
 I'll smile. I'll say thank you.
 But honestly?
 If I don't feel your heart in it, it won't stay with me.

But get me something simple, random, even silly-
 like a wildflower you saw while walking home,
 or a pack of imli toffees because you remembered I mentioned them once months ago-
 and I swear, you'll find me holding onto it like its gold.
 Like it means the world.

Because it does.

I'm built that way.
 I don't fall for price tags.

I fall for moments.
For people who listen even when I don't realize I'm speaking.
For people who pick up on the little things and carry them quietly.

When I give gifts, I do the same.
I sit.
I think.
I remember that one random thing you said at 2 AM.
I brainstorm for days.
I bake you your favorite cake because you once told me it reminds you of home.
I make parathas when you're low.
I find that one scent that feels like you.

And maybe these things don't come in shiny boxes.
Maybe they don't come with big brand names.
But every single one carries pieces of me.

That's why it stings so much when people don't see it.
When they unwrap my gift and wonder how much it cost,
as if my love is measured in currency.
As if thought doesn't count.

It hurts.
Because I wasn't giving them "a gift".
I was giving them a part of my heart I had carefully, quietly, stitched together.

Not everyone gets it.
I've made my peace with that, mostly.
Some people need grand gestures and big price tags to feel seen.
And that's okay.

But if you're someone whose heart smiles at the small things-
 At the remembered details, the inside jokes, the late-night
cravings I quietly fulfill-
 then you get it.

You're my kind of person.

And if I find you, we're a team.
 Because for us, love never came wrapped in ribbons.
 It came tucked inside the smallest gestures.

And that?
 That is priceless.

16. I Can't Say Thankyou

For some reason, I've never been able to say *thank you* when it truly matters.

When someone lends me a pen, when someone holds the door, when someone passes me a glass of water - the words come out so easily.
 "Thank you."
 Soft. Effortless. Almost automatic.

But when it comes to the things that touch my heart - the things that shake something inside me, that make my chest ache with emotions I can't name - the words abandon me completely.

It's strange, isn't it?
 The bigger the feeling, the heavier those two simple words become.
 They sit there, heavy and trembling at the back of my throat, like a bird that refuses to fly.
 No matter how much I want to release them, they stay trapped.
 Silent.

And because of that, people often think I'm ungrateful.
 That I don't appreciate things.
 That I'm too proud, too cold, too self-absorbed to acknowledge what people do for me.
 They don't understand, and honestly, I never really did either.
 For years, I kept wondering: *Why can't I say it?*
 Why does gratitude feel heavier than pain?

And then one day, it happened.
I saw *him*.

Sitting across from me at a small table by the window.
The world moved around us - waiters, lights, clinking glasses - but his eyes stayed on me.
And in those eyes, I saw it - everything.
Every emotion I had felt inside myself for so long, reflected right back at me.

Gratitude.
Relief.
Love.
Comfort.
Fear.
Hope.
All tangled together, layered over each other like soft waves.

He didn't say anything.
No words.
No *thank you*.
But he didn't have to.
Because I saw it.
I felt it.
Every bit of unspoken gratitude sat in that silence between us.

And in that moment, something inside me finally made sense.
That's what I've been doing all along.

I've been thanking people with my silences.
With the way I hold eye contact just a little longer.
With the way my hands tremble when I try to find the right words but fail.
With the way I replay their kindness in my mind for days,

holding on to it like a secret gift.
 With the way I quietly show up for them when they least expect it.
 With the way I remember every little thing they've done for me, even years later.

My gratitude has never lived in my words.
 It's lived in my heart.
 It's lived in the way I hold people, even when I don't hold their hands.
 It's lived in the way I listen, in the way I silently pray for them, in the way I hope they find happiness even if I don't get to witness it.

But the world doesn't always know how to read silences.
 The world wants words.
 And because my gratitude isn't loud, they call it absence.
 Because my gratitude isn't spoken, they call it ingratitude.

But not him.
 He didn't need the words.
 Because he carried the same weight.
 He knew exactly how gratitude can fill you to the brim, and still leave you speechless.

Some people say thank you with words.
 Some say it with grand gestures.
 But some of us - we say it with our eyes, our quiet presence, our stubborn loyalty, our gentle patience.

And maybe that's why life made me sit across from him that day - to show me that my way of loving, of thanking, of feeling - is not wrong.

It's just quiet.
It's just *mine*.

The world may never notice.
But those who are meant for me, will always know.

QARAAR

17. Ilhaam

Standing in a queue,

I was thinking about you.

Try focus on why you came today-

Not let the heart just drift away.

My heart insisted you were near,

My mind kept laughing, "He's not here."

I told myself, "Stop feeling much,

This isn't love-just a memory's touch."

But the line moved up, and so did I,

Still battling thought, still asking why,

When suddenly, through the shifting view-

There you were... and time withdrew.

Red sweatshirt, hand upon your face,

Drowning deep in a silent space.

I stared, unsure if you were real,

Or made up of my heart's appeals.

Till you looked up-your gaze met mine,

Turned your body towards me.

Hand still resting on your cheek,

Your smile said things you didn't speak.

You lit up like a child might do

On seeing someone they never outgrew.

And I? I froze-completely tossed,

In that joy, I was somehow lost.

I didn't hear the crowd behind,

Didn't notice the noise unwind.

Till you signed at me with gentle grace,

Bringing me back to time and place.

My specs slipped down from nervous hands,

You were there, I was trying to understand.

I was too lost in your quiet gaze,

Too caught in that soft haze.

And later still, you walked my way,

The moment stretched but wouldn't stay.

Someone called me, and I turned,

But not before my heartbeat burned.

I saw the dust rise from your shoes,

As if time paused and let me choose.

Not grand, not loud, no skies of blue-

Just you, just me and a fading view.

To a moment simple, strange, and true-

When I stood in a queue,

And was found by you.

18. Guava Chilli Mojito

She saw him - sitting at the corner table near the glass wall, waiting, looking at her with those eyes.
 An hour late is too much, some would say.
 But love never measures time in minutes.
 Though he does.
 For him, let's just say - the wait felt worthy.

The moment she entered, he stood up instinctively.
 His arms twitched slightly, almost rising for an embrace, but she pretended not to notice.
 It wasn't rudeness - it was restraint.
 She couldn't afford to melt into his arms.
 Not now. Not so soon.
 Because she knew - the moment she would feel his warmth, everything carefully held inside her chest would crumble, and those tears she locked away would finally betray her.

This wasn't the first time she did this...
 The last time they met, sitting beside her, he had opened his hand like he always would - inviting her fingers into his.
 Back then too, she had used all her willpower to resist holding his hand.

So now, she kept talking and gently slipped into the seat across from him.
 They sat there, meeting after months - no, not just months - after years of waiting for life to finally make space for them.

This meeting wasn't casual.
 It wasn't even about this day.
 It was a moment that had been waiting for them since the day

they first exchanged glances, when destiny quietly whispered,
"Your story has just begun."

Their souls danced - light teasing, warm laughter, stolen
glances, and long pauses heavy with unsaid emotions.
 They flirted.
 They blushed.
 Though if she asked him, he'd blame the pinkness of his cheeks
on the guava chili mojito.

At one point, he reached across the table, pretending to check if
his pen was working - as if there weren't any napkins or
notepads lying right there.
 His fingers held her index finger - gently, deliberately.

"Ullu..." she whispered under her breath when he let go after
checking the pen.
 She didn't pull her hand away.
 That idiot did.
 Why did he?
 Why let go, when his fingers had finally found their way to
hers?

That night - silly, beautiful, sacred night - she went to bed
without washing her hand.
 The faint ink stain on her finger wasn't just ink; it was his
imprint - fragile, invisible, but deeply present.
 And she was determined to hold on to it, for just a little longer.

Strange, aren't they?
 These two - who never agree they love each other, yet love
each other in silence.
 Finding poetry in glances, in fingertips barely touching.
 Speaking in a language that needs no words.

 Hugging the pillow tighter to sleep, as if it carries the warmth of each other's absence.
 Turning every conversation into a fight, yet somehow always standing on each other's side.
 Loving in the most complicated, imperfect, yet truest way.

19. "I Love You"

I don't believe in *I love you*,
 not like most people do.
 Those words fall off tongues too fast,
 like promises not meant to last.

I've heard them tossed in passing breeze,
 like morning greetings, casual ease.
 Empty sounds that people say,
 when hearts aren't brave enough to stay.

But love-real love-it's not that light,
 it's heavy, keeps you up at night.
 It sits like weight upon your chest,
 it lives in silence, not confessed.

So I don't say it, I just show,
 in quiet ways you may not know.
 In tiny things I keep in mind,
 in words you dropped, I went to find.

I fight with you, I tease, I play,
 I crack dumb jokes throughout the day.
 I send you voice notes late at night,
 just to make sure your heart feels light.

I hold my tongue when anger flares,
 I guard my words, because I care.
 One wrong word can scar like flame,
 and I can't bear to bring you pain.

I sit beside you, saying none,
 when storms arrive, I let them run.

No need for answers, no quick mend,
just me, beside you, till it ends.

I don't complain to those outside,
 your flaws, in me, I safely hide.
 How can I tell the world your wrong,
 when to God, I pray you stay strong?

"Heal him, if You must," I pray,
 "But please, in gentle, kinder ways."
 "Keep him safe and let him grow,
 but never break what makes him glow."

You won't hear it loud from me,
 in words as light as air can be.
 But you'll see it if you watch close,
 in every little thing I chose.

In screenshots saved, in poems i post,
 where your reflection isn't lost.
 In the way my eyes don't pull away,
 and how I hope you feel what I won't say.

So no, I don't believe in words alone,
 in hollow phrases overthrown.
 My love lives where my silence grew...
 not loud, not perfect...
 but always true.

20.Imperfect

You're not perfect.
Neither am I.
We both carry flaws we can't deny.
I say too much, you say too few,
I pull you in, you push me through.

I talk in circles, emotions wide,
You hide your storms somewhere inside.
Your silence speaks, my words explode,
Two broken souls on one shared road.

The insecurities, the heavy air,
The quiet fights we sometimes bear.
Some wounds we've seen, some still to find,
But through the mess, I never mind.

Because if I must live in any mess,
Let it be this, I must confess.
If life is flawed and full of rain,
Let me dance with you in the pain.

If I must sink, I'll sink in you,
Your arms my ocean, steady and true.
If I must break, let it be near,
The hands that hold me when I fear.

There'll be nights we lose our way,
Sit in silence, with nothing to say.
But even then, I'll still choose you,
Not for ease - but because it's true.

Not because you're flawless bright,
 But because you're worth the fight.
 Your worst is still my favorite place,
 Your broken parts, my softest grace.

If the world must pull apart,
 Let me break with you, heart to heart.
 If I must learn and fall once more,
 Let me fall through your open door.

I don't love you for perfect days,
 I love your chaos, your tangled ways.
 Your flaws, your cracks, your wild, your wrong,
 In your mess is where I belong.

And know this too - it's not my style,
 With others, I lose my warmth and smile.
 Their mess annoys, I walk away,
 But yours - I write my poems and stay.

I don't know why I love you so,
 Why for you, I bend and glow.
 It's never been like this before,
 I open doors I'd shut before.

The grace I give, the space I make,
 For you, it flows, it doesn't break.
 It's like my heart just knows its cue -
 To stretch, to hold, to fit just you.

21. Home

I kept on searching in places unknown,
 For a feeling, a corner, a place of my own.
 I chased every trace, every place, every park,
 Hoping for a place that'd light up my dark.

I wanted a place I could run to each night,
 After long tiring days, after wrongs and fights.
 When dreams felt heavy or when sleep stayed away,
 A place I'd return to at the end of each day.

Then one day I sat beside a boy so still,
 His eyes held a shine, like stars that fill.
 And unknowingly, something begun,
 Without a warning - I had found the one.

I found myself running to him with a treat,
 Bringing small joys, simple and sweet.
 I fight with him more times than I can count,
 Yet always return- like hearts always mount.

It wasn't just me, no, he feels it too,
 In his little ways, he pulls me through.
 We fight, we laugh, we stumble, we fall,
 Yet somehow, together, we conquer it all.
 But even in the breaking, we both know -
 There's no place else we'd rather go.

Because home isn't built with perfect days,
 It's found in hearts that choose to stay.

And somehow, in your arms, I've found mine -
Without even knowing, without a sign.

You feel like home - simple and true,
A place I'll keep running back to.
In every fight, in every fall -
You're my forever, my all in all.

Ikhtitam

As you turn these final pages,
I hope you don't just love
I hope you learn to nurture it.
To hold it gently, to protect it softly.
Because love lives in small moments
In quiet understanding, in shared silences,
In the simple act of choosing each other over and over
again(even on the days you wanna kill them).
And if ever life feels heavy,
May you always find your way back
To the comfort of each other's hearts,
To the Essence that first brought you here.

And when you look at them, may your heart softly says:

"Then which of the favors of your Lord will you deny?"
(Surah Ar-Rahman, 55:13)